Lathom Junior School

Young Writers and Illustrators

Published by New Generation Publishing in 2024

Paperback ISBN: 9781835632864

New Generation Publishing
www.newgeneration-publishing.com

Foreword

As Executive Headteacher of Lathom Junior School, it gives me great pleasure to present this book of poems, rhymes and short stories written and composed by children and staff. I congratulate everyone who has contributed, especially Kitty, Ms Clairmont, whose initial idea, infectious excitement and endless energy has resulted in this beautiful collated collection.

We love writing at our school and children proudly share their words and thoughts at every opportunity, discussing their compositions and describing their illustrations confidently. Our staff are wonderful role models for the children. Thanks to them, our children have confident voices with which to eloquently express their ideas.

Sarah Rowlands

INTRODUCTION

Budding young writers and artists from Lathom Junior School have poured precious hours into these works to bring forth their dreams, hopes and aspirations to be shared and celebrated with you in these pages. They embody the very best of what anyone could hope for in our new generation, I hope they will inspire you in turn.

Kitty Clairmont

CONTENTS

Year 4

Fariha: Bestie
Muhammad: Dragons
Roshni: Yacht
Ezekiel: I want to be a superhero
Menaal: Sailing
Aradhana: The Lonely Bird
Arnia: The frog
Inaya: Tiger
Zarrish: What an adventure
Aayan: Animals
Aisha: Cyberbullying
Avenian: How the Crystal Moves

Year 5

Nilima: The Poem of the messengers of Islam
Nilima: Learning
Kabinaya: Dreams
Anabia: Umbrella
Nilima: Teacher
Stephanie: The Solar System
Stephanie: A New Year
Rukser: A True Friend
Sagana: Diwali
Sagana: Mango
Elsa: Lathom Junior School
Nifa: Sunflower
Ifra: Life

Year 6

Hasina: *Flower*
Lashana: *Never Give Up*
Hashina: *Kindness*
Sai: *Transition*
Hania: *Butterfly*

Haresa: *All about Life*
Aylah: *Kindness*
Amelia: *War*
Amelia: *Cats*
Arissa: *Life*
Apitam: *School Life*
Kansika: *Black Lives Matter*
Kansika: *Life*
Divyansh: *Fruit*
Fareeha: *Racism*
Rithuna: *Life*
Mithusa: *Hidden Secrets*
Mithusa: *The Abandoned House*
Mahreen: *The Values*

Phoenix: **Victoria Lockhart**

Through resilience, great things are reborn – Kitty

Kindness

Khaled Subhan

Kindness brings people together
When someone is sad and upset
Just saying hello makes them feel better
We all have good days and bad days
But always remember with hardship comes ease
In a world where you can be anyone,
Be kind, caring and be at peace

LATHOM

Yolanda Musinguzi

Lathom Lathom Lathom
A school like no other.

A school where the children laugh.
A school where the children get messy.
A school where the children dance the Flamenco.
A school where we break world records.
A school where we play chess and win trophies.
A school where cheerleaders are made.

Lathom Lathom Lathom
Unique in every way

A school where many hands from many lands are clasped in
friendship true.
A school where the parents are warmly welcomed.
A school that makes us think and dream.
A school where everyone makes it a safe and happy place.
This is our school where we are all happy and love to learn.

ADOPTED

Navina Prakash

One summer's day
She wandered into our little garden
Yowling and howling she came
Hungry and afraid

My little girl saw her first
This tiny, mewling little being
We were cautious and so was she
Bit by bit
Step by step
We welcomed her into our home
And into our hearts

When young she would
Run and play a lot
Climb our cherry blossom tree
Walk up and down the wooden fence
And stand guard on our garden patio

Older now
She sleeps much more
Is less excitable, less curious
More content and habitual

She likes fresh cream on cakes,
Warm custard,
Grated strong cheddar,
Nibbles on pieces of brioche but
She's partial to peanut butter – the smooth kind!

Over the years, fifteen to count
She's rooted herself into our family
Sharing our ups and downs
She is our constant
Our friend, our confidant
Our mackerel striped tabby called
Twinkles

FLIGHT OF MIGRATION

Sabina Khanam

As the crystal clear dew drops glisten in the morning light,
The air fills its expansion with the glorious sun so bright.

Free flowing birds, gracefully swoon high and low,
Tweeting, chirping, cheerfully through the skyline glow.
Looking for a precious place to call their own,
Gliding, then soaring high as they roam,
What a tremendous and wondrous sight to see!
Under the blanket of green layered maple tree,
They eloquently pause and quietly settle,
Choosing this a place to call their own.

As the day comes to an end, it is clear to perceive that the journey
we take is the reward of our diligence!
Yet, we deliberate, contemplate and doubt what we venture to achieve
When in the end what matters is, what you and I choose to really believe!

TEACHER

Kitty Clairmont

Long hours under a lamp
Realms of papers underarm
Sleepless nights and belly taut
Their progress a soothing balm

A conductor of learning
To an orchestra of eyes
Sparkling bright and awaiting
The crescendo on its rise

Nervous twitches on some mouths
Others keen to share a thought
Tentative answers reach up
Imaginatively caught

Manoeuvring moves to bass
Trombones and clarinets now
Fine tuning the violins
Find room for the drums but how?

But just as chaos threatens
Like a light upon the shore
The orchestra join as one
And confusion is no more

The wrong answer is sighing
But the right answer now cheers
And a melody now sings
Chasing away all the fears

Applause for the conductor
The conductor takes a bow
Turning to the orchestra
Salutes them and makes a vow

As long as you will need me
Right here is where I belong
Bass and treble clef are we
For without you there is no song

Lathom School Values

Holly Class

Kind Kiera is all about kindness
So no-one feels alone
Never bully anyone
And be kind to all

Communicative Catrina
Is all about how we speak to people
Communicate clearly
And choose your words carefully

Reflective Rashid is about how we think
About our behaviour and attitude
Take the time to think about
What you can improve

Resilient Ronald never gives up
Keep trying to achieve what you want
Remember to ask for help too
And don't let anyone put you off

Confident Ketan is about believing in yourself
Even if you are nervous or scared
Try your best all the time
That is good enough

Curious Cashini is about wanting to learn
Finding out about different things
Can really be fun
With other people or on your own

Rule of Lathom Junior

Holly Class

Attendance is important – 100% please
Unless you are very sick or have a deadly disease

Rules for behaviour, no bullies here
We believe in respect, no fear only cheer

Democracy, we have plenty of roles
To be school councillors, buddies or mediators are our goals

We represent and look after each other
As a family, like a sister or a brother

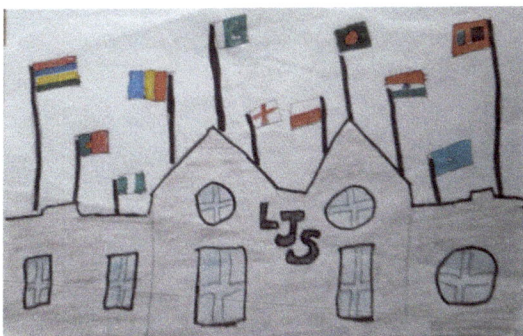

Lathom Junior School: **Maha** yr3

HAPPINESS

Jennah

Happiness, happiness
Makes me feel good
It's a bright yellow ball in the sky
When I am moving
I say good bye
Spending time with my family
Playing with my cat when I cuddle her
Happiness is a lovely smile on your face.

Cat: **Arissa** yr5

FEAR

Hadhiq

Being scared is not good
Don't be scared, I'm here
Wolves, foxes, bears and dogs
It doesn't matter
If you're scared I'm beside you
Remember

Friends: **Aathmika** yr3

CALM

Ziad

Calmness is the colour green
It is sitting calmly under a tree
It is a beautiful orange flower

Garden: **Hafsa** yr3

HAPPINESS

Elizah

Happiness is having fun.
I like to dance. I like pink.
Happiness is a yellow bright sun.
I love doing math. I love reading.
Happiness is playing with my baby sister.
It's going on a school trip.

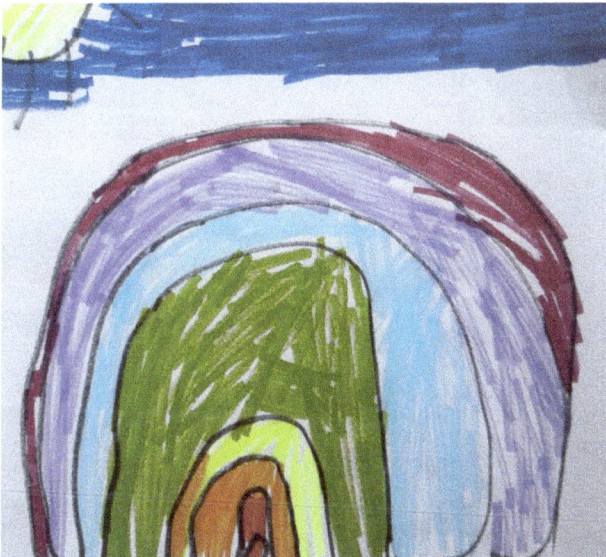

Happiness: **Aathmika** yr3

CALMNESS

Kiran

Calmness is:
a white feather from a bird
being left alone and no one bothering me
reading a book in a quiet corner
giving someone a warm hug
going to rest in bed.

Peaceful: **Stephanie** yr5

TIGER

Hazel Class

Just as the tiger stepped out of his lair
Up he looked and saw a flash of lightening
Night time it was, and in fear he was shaking
Gnashing his teeth to the sound of thunder
The tiger's fear kept growing stronger
Lightning strikes
Heart pounds
Tiger's head hits the ground.
Eventually, growling through his fear
He wanted to disappear
But found the courage to reappear!

Tiger: **Hira** yr4

POTATO

Arain

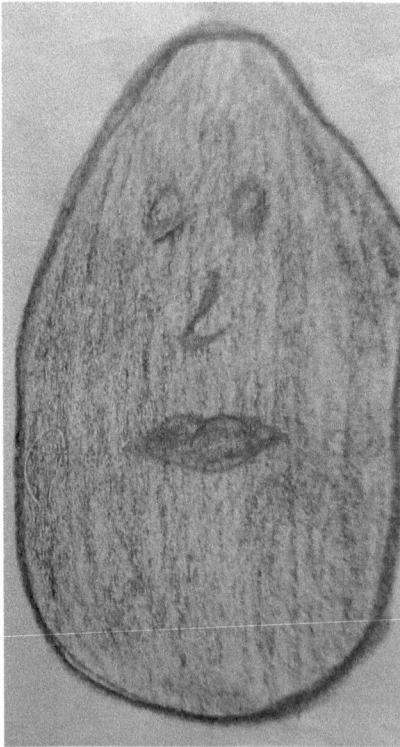

Potato: **Arain** yr3

Hi, I'm a potato. I was born in a dark place and the first time I saw light, it was the time when a human took me out from the dark and put me in a basket where I saw lots of potatoes like me. Then they loaded us in a truck and after a few hours we entered a chips factory. They gave us a good bath which was funny, then they peeled us. I cried a lot, it was painful. Then they cut us brutally. I cried a lot. They gave us another bath and put us in hot oil. My whole body burned. They packed me in a bag and it was dark again. I saw light when a human opened the bag but it was my last light because he ate me.

UMAIRA

The Rainbow

Once upon a time there was a magnificent rainbow. It would come every time it rained and when it was sunny, it was beautiful to watch. One day it didn't rain and wasn't sunny so the rainbow didn't come out. People were so sad, "The beautiful rainbow is gone!" But one day it rained heavily then suddenly it was sunny again.

"It is a miracle!" people laughed. They were skipping and laughing, they were so happy. They began rushing out of their houses in a flash and sat down together to watch the rainbow.

Rainbow: **Inaaya** yr3

THE CHEESE AND THE MOUSE

Ioana

The mouse was a very small animal and it loved cheese. It loved cheese so much but it took only a small bite out of the cheese then hid it. The next day, the cheese was gone! He was very sad. He couldn't stop thinking about the cheese. He searched everywhere and then he saw it! He saw the cheese but it was walking towards him. He was finally happy but it felt weird now being friends with the cheese.

You probably thought the mouse would stop thinking about cheese now and he did.

Mouse and Cheese: **Ioana** yr3

A MAN'S BEST FRIEND

Tayon

Dog: **Stephanie** yr5

This is a story about a man and a dog. The man's name is Ronald and he owned a pet shop. The dog's name is George and is now living in the pet shop Ronald owned. They had a close relationship. Ronald had found George all alone in an alley way, waiting for somebody to help him but nobody did, except for Ronald. He saw George and couldn't just let him stay there so he took him as his own pet. He put him in the pet stop until he could get himself a real house. He lived in a flat but he was low on rent and he didn't have enough room.

He tried everything but no luck. He started telling everyone who came into the pet shop about George. So many people came to hear the story that he was able to buy himself a real house. George finally got to live with him. Ten years later, Ronald became a multimillionaire and him and George had a wonderful life!

FLOWERS

Sarina

Flowers: Stephanie yr5

Flowers are so beautiful
Any flower could have power
Even a baby one
Imagine if a flower only lived for an hour
I love pretty flowers
A flower is almost grass
A flower showers in the rain
Flowers are my favourite plant!
Can't they be your favourite plant?

PHOENIX

Uthessman

Wings
Fiery, brave
Speedy, invisible, magical
Mythical, invincible, indestructible
destroying

Phoenix: **Victoria Lockhart**

Rainbows

Inaaya

Rainbows are colourful
Artists paint a lot of rainbows
I love rainbows so much
They're my favourite
When people see a rainbow they feel happy
Because they are very magical
Only when the sun is shining and it rains the rainbow forms
When will I see a rainbow again?

Rainbow: **Sagana** yr5

FLOWERS

Akshara

Flowers are nice
I love them
Do you like them? Which ones?
Some are pink, red, yellow and white
Also many more mixtures of colours
As long as you water them
They will grow nice and big

Flowers: **Akshara** yr3

LATHOM

Thejesh

Lathom Junior School
A lovely school
The wonderful class I'm in
Happiness is everywhere
Oh…I forgot my reading record!
My school family is kind

Just for one day you're missing your playtime
Ummmm…I've got an idea
Now can I be your friend?
I can be kind
Or should I be a line monitor?
Rules have to be followed

School teacher is kind
Can you help me please?
Helping everyone
Oh my gosh!
Oops! I forgot my homework!
Lathom, I love it here

SCHOOL REFLECTION

Maha

This is our school
May we all live happily together
May we work hard
May we be kind to one another
May love dwell here
May love of people everywhere
May love of life itself
May everyone make this school a safe and happy place

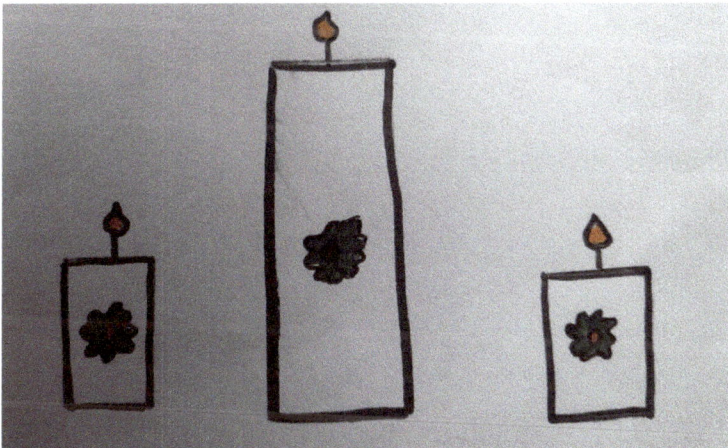

Candles: **Maha** yr3

MY SCHOOL

Maha

Lathom Junior School in East Ham
Amazing children in each class
Tall buildings almost till the sky
High stairs to climb to the top
Our school is full of cool teachers
My teacher is very nice

Joyful trips we get to go to
Underline the date and LO
Never forget your reading record
Interesting and new things we learn
Oranges for desert
Raising money for different charities

School starts on Monday and ends on Friday
Caring for one another everywhere
Having fun with your teachers and friends
Our school is full of displays
Open the gate for children to come in
Learn your times tables on TTRS and shine at Lathom Junior School.

SONG

Sabeen

Dreams come from your heart
and you wanna say: This is my dream!
 Oooh oh that is a big dream!
Say I want it to come true!
Never let it go away
You need it, this is your dream
So let it come true!
Yaa-aa-a so let it come true
Never give up on your dream!
You want it so go get it
Let your heart show your dream
I wanna see it so you will be freeee!
Show me your dreee-eeam!
I wanna see it.
This is my dream.

Dream: **Sabeen** yr3

TOLERANCE

Hornbeam Class

Tolerating other people's faiths and beliefs

Other people's choices are their choices to make

Learn about other people's beliefs and listen

Everyone can accept and celebrate each other's differences

Respect other people, no matter how different they are

A good person who tolerates everyone is a great person

Not accepting someone's differences will make them sad

Caring for others is a great thing, so accept them

Equally sharing and tolerating each other is a British Value

BESTIE

Fariha

Roses are red
Violets are blue
This is my world
Where I met you

Dream: **Afrin** yr5

DRAGONS

Muhammad

Dragons
Aggressive, piercing
Ominous, sinister, hateful
Petrifying, blazing, blood-thirsty
mythical

Dragon: **Yousraa** yr4

YACHT

Roshni

Above the waves, the glorious sun burned the whole ocean
As the sun set, the turbulent waves splashed as loud as thunder
Beneath the clouds, the sails sailed as fast as a marathon
Around the waves, the yacht zoomed across the sea
Underneath the sea, an enormous unknown creature dashed by
On the gigantic yacht, a black and white Dalmatian
Whined repeatedly in fear

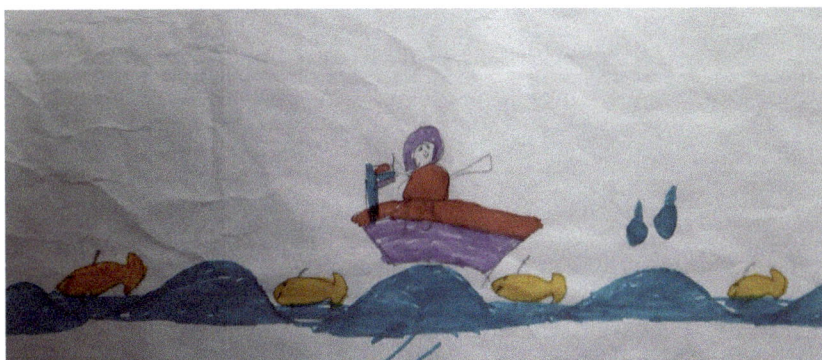

Sailing: **Kambo** yr4

I WANT TO BE A SUPERHERO

Ezekiel

I want to be a superhero
Because I want to save people
And blast my enemies to zero
So everyone can be equal

I want to be a superhero
Because I want to show my super powers
But I can't tell anyone I am a hero
It's lonely when I jump over towers
I want to be a superhero
Because it's my only wish
Maybe I can have a cool gizmo
But I can't be a superhero….or can I ?

SAILING

Menaal

Above the waves, the sun glowed till
The sea was covered in light

Around the waves, the yacht swished
In the wind slowly

In the distance, the mountains waved
Goodbye from above

In the heavens above the clouds
Calmly moved at the speed of a snail

THE LONELY BIRD

Aradhana

Once upon a time, there was a bird and it was always lonely.
    One day the lonely bird was crying and everyone noticed.
    Then the lonely bird looked at everybody.
    The everybody started to stare at the bird.
    Then the lonely bird flew away.
    While the bird was flying, it fell to the ground and…died.

Bird: **Jasmina** yr4

THE FROG

Arnia

Frog: **Ahmad** yr4

Once upon a time, there was a girl named Daisy who had a frog that disturbed her a lot. One day the girl lost the frog and she felt so happy. But she kept hearing strange noises. So she checked the whole house just to make sure it wasn't the frog but she didn't see anyone except her mum, dad and sister called Rosey. She enjoyed the peace until the next day when her sister Rosey asked, "Where is the frog?"

Daisy answered, "It's gone!"

"Mum is going to so mad!" Rosey warned.

"Maybe it's still here, I keep hearing voices like ribbit, ribbit!" said Daisy nervously.

Oh! That was me!" laughed Rosey, "I was copying our frog!"

"Oh no! What am I going to do?"

TIGER

Inaya

Terrified, hungry tiger
Dark, wet rainforest
Sharp, spikey vines
Spooky, dark grey sky
Loud, heavy rain
Fierce, petrifying thunder
Slimy, wet leaves
Spikey, old, bendy tree
Slimy, wet branches
Wet, cold leaves
Sharp, rough claws

Tiger: **Iliada** yr4

WHAT AN ADVENTURE

Zarrish

"Don't press the button!" yelled a voice. But it was too late. Luke had already pressed that ruby red button.

"No! you will kill us all! Remember stay away from green goblins!" This time it was clear that it was a grumpy old man's voice.

All of a sudden, Jack and Lucy, who were brother and sister, felt the ground beneath them collapse. All they could feel for a moment was gone as they floated in mid-air.

"Where are we?" asked Lucy curiously as she brushed off the dust.

"Don't ask me! It's not like I've been here before!" replied Jack feeling annoyed.

From out of the bushes, the children heard a rustling sound and instantly remembered what the old man had said. It was a goblin! As they ran for their lives they bumped into a dead-end but they couldn't stop there so they climbed over to the other side. Another dead-end!

"Don't eat me! I'm not tasty, I'm smelly!" cried Jack, flinging his arms around.

Beep, beep, beep sounded the alarm. Looks like it was a dream! What an adventure! That dream was quite peculiar!

ANIMALS

Aayan

Animals are amazing creatures
The come in all shapes, sizes and features
Some are furry, some are scaly and some are slimy
Some are friendly, some are scary and some are tiny

Animals live in different habitats
Forest, oceans, deserts and sometimes even on people's mats
Bats hang upside down and live in the dark
Dogs stay at home or go outside and bark

Animals have different methods of communication
Sounds, gestures, colour even vibration
There are a mixture of types of animals
Mammals, carnivores, herbivores and reptiles

CYBERBULLYING

Aisha

If you ever get bullied online
Tell a trusted adult or parent every time

If you are in a game and your friend makes fun of you
This is what you should do…
tell someone

If anyone on a game asks for personal info
don't tell them anything – just go

If during a game things are said that are bad
Block –report- tell your mum and dad

If your friend sends a photo of you online looking like a fool
That's bullying – that's not cool

How the Crystal Moves

Avenian

One day, Mr Gem bought a crystal. It moved 1cm. It was moving slowly, slowly. It didn't stop at all. On the day Mr Gem spotted the crystal move, he thought it was a dream. But it wasn't. It really happened. He searched it up on Google. It had happened because the crystal had melted and the strong water was carrying it. It was all his fault! He had accidentally bought a melting crystal. He threw the crystal in the bin. Weird and funny he thought.

The Poem of the messengers of Islam

Nilima

Messengers and prophets were many in number
Sent down from one God, the Almighty Creator
From Adam to Muhammad, peace be upon them
Shone in this world, more than diamonds and gems
Islam is what they taught
The truth is what they brought
Each of them was outstanding
Their qualities were amazing
They were far above all
Towards Allah they did call

LEARNING

Nilima

I wake up in the morning
Tired as a sloth
I go to school
Textbooks piled high on the table
I want to escape

I enter a new world
Meet new people
Visit places
Learn new things
Every time I open a book

When I learn my brain becomes stronger
When I explore the realms of subjects, I discover a new world
When I go to school I learn a lot
I'll never give up
A cross will never hold me back

DREAMS

Kabinaya

Doing the things you love
Running around while exploring your dreams
Enjoying the time of our imagination
And most importantly having fun
Making your wishes come true
Spinning and twirling in your dream place

UMBRELLA

Anabia

My umbrella is so bright
So bright, so bright
It stops water leaking on my head, head, head
My umbrella is so bright, blue, yellow, red and white
It keeps the raindrops off my head, head, head

Umbrella: **Zahra** yr4

Teacher

Nilima

Partner checker
Rule setter
Education giver
Quick thinker
Smart educator
Care giver
Praise giver
Natural orator
Corridor stalker
Inspiring mentor

THE SOLAR SYSTEM

Stephanie

The solar system is made of many things
Stars, dwarf planets and planets with rings
The big eight: Mars, Venus, Earth and Mercury
Jupiter, Saturn, Uranus, Neptune…
What happened to poor Pluto?
Only a dwarf planet as it is so tiny
Oh wow the stars are shiny!

Solar System: **Sephanie** yr5

A NEW YEAR

Stephanie

It's the new year, a worldwide celebration
Fireworks are being lit by more than half the nation
At midnight the chaos starts with animals hiding away
Popping crackling from the sky
Oh look! It's time to say our last 2023 goodbye
A wild and wide crowd waiting in front of the London Eye
Now 2024 says hi!
Screaming, cheering all around the world for 2024
The grey, gloomy sky filled with smoke
An unforgettable day

Fireworks: **Nifa** yr5

A TRUE FRIEND

Rukser

Your friendship
Is something called a special gift
And I hope you know I care for you
More than these letters together can say
And the next time I see you
I'll say Hey!

DIWALI

Sagana

Diwali is the festival of lights
In our homes we will put rangoli patterns to welcome happiness
We welcome Rama and Sita
Add diva lamps to light the way home
Late at night, fireworks launch into the sky
In the evening, people go to temple to celebrate

MANGO

Sagana

Mangos are fruits
And are ripe in summer
Nectar can come from the fruit's flowers
Grand mangos are giant mangos and even
On a sunny day, they could be ready to eat

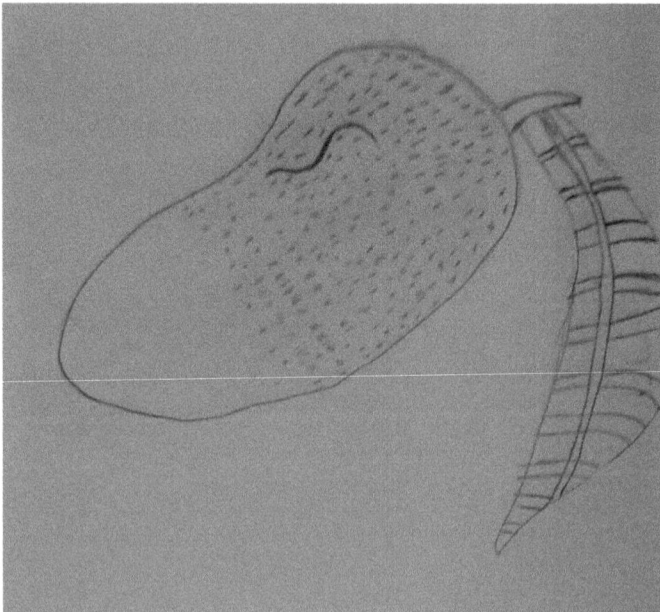

Mango: **Jasmina** yr4

LATHOM JUNIOR SCHOOL

Elsa

Laughter and cheering sounds is what I hear in the playground
Amazing presentation and work is what is expected
Teachers give their students a valuable education
Helping others is a good choice
Outstanding behaviour is what is expected
Memories are made that will last for forever

Joyful children are what the school loves to see
Unique individuals make school so bright and creative
No one is meant to feel left out because we have buddy experts
Intelligent is what we become
Obstacles are never a problem because our teachers guide us
Reading gives you knowledge and helps you find new vocabulary

Singing is what we do in school
Confidence is what the children encourage themselves to have
Hard work always pays off
Opportunities are what you have in Lathom Junior School
Our versatile hall is used for PE, fairs and lunch
Listening skills are essential when learning which is what we do best

SUNFLOWER

Nifa

Sparkling stars make my eye glow in the cold breeze.
The sun sets slowly down on my head
Saying
Goodbye.

When the sun rises you can see
Me smile at you with my bright yellow
I will give you a warm hug
Whenever you need.

Sunflowers: **Jessica** yr6

LIFE

Ifra

You make me happy
You make me sad
You make me mad
You make me glad

You make me feel like anything is possible

I look up
I look down
I look left
I look right

But now I want to run from reality
I want to crawl into a hole and stay there for eternity
Then you told me that it will be okay
So I let go of my fear to struggle today
Don't give up and don't give in
The end is just the beginning

FLOWER

Hasina

Flowers bloom every spring
Awakened by the shiny sunshine
Now that it is winter time
Where is my lovely spring time?
Oh flower! Oh flower! Where are you?
I have been looking for you
Where are you?

Flower: **Hasina** yr6

NEVER GIVE UP

Lashana

Restlessness of putting all your effort is not a waste
Endless amount of trying will never be useless
So be resilient and never give up
It'll be fine and never give up
Lots of efforts into your work will bring success
Be consistent in all your work, put all the effort that you can
Consistency will build your success and confidence
Never give up, never surrender
Resilience can be a wave throughout your life
Even though you may suffer never give up

Kindness

Hashina

Kindness is true
Kindness doesn't make you blue
A little bit of kindness can spread across the world
Everyone should do the same

Every kind word
Could embrace the world
Be kind no matter what
The world would be a better place

Bless people with kindness
Love everyone
Kindness is a strong word
It can help people

Be happy and be kind
Make sure to be kind next time
Kindness can spread throughout the world
Uniting everyone

Transition

Sai

In primary school, I had fun with my friends
But moving to secondary, I'll lose them all
In primary school, I had caring teachers
But moving to secondary, I don't know who I'll get
In primary, I had a warm welcome into school
But in secondary, I might meet bullies
Who will I have caring for me
When we're moving to secondary?
I will miss my friends from primary
But life just moves on into secondary school

BUTTERFLY

Honia

Butterfly, butterfly
Fly away so
Far and high
Spread your wings, spread them wide
Flap until you can fly
Butterfly, butterfly
Your wings will shine
Very bright

Butterfly: **Aathmika** yr3

ALL ABOUT LIFE

Haresa

Life can be beautiful
Life can be kind
Sometimes
Life can be rude
Life can be hurtful
Life can be everything

KINDNESS

Aylah

In a world that can be tough and unkind
A little act of kindness is what we need
A smile or a hello
Can make someone's day brighter you know?

Kindness is like a ripple in a pond
Spreading love and warmth beyond
It starts with one
But grows and grows
Touching hearts wherever it goes

So let's be kind every single day
In our words and actions in every way
For kindness is a gift we all can share

Butterfly: **Sabina** yr4

WAR

Amelia

Stop fighting like cats and dogs
We need peace in this world
Peace, I say
Stop the war in Gaza
I miss the good old days
The days when there was no war
When there was freedom
Oh how beautiful is freedom
Save the children please
How would you feel if this was on your doorstep?

CATS

Amelia

I love cats
Oh how cute and fluffy they are
And very cuddly
Their faces are the cutest
Their ears give me the best feeling in the world
Oh how I love cats

Cat: **Catalin** yr3

LIFE

Arissa

Life is just a collection of stories from the past
No matter what you do
You'll always get consequences
Don't let life overcome you
One day you'll be the person who has regrets
Therefore just remember to embrace yourself
You'll never be at this point in your life again

SCHOOL LIFE

Apitam

Growing up in my school
Learning is exciting
Reading and maths are fun and
writing can be like drawing

Every single child has the strength to reach their full potential
With the support of the teacher
anything is possible

When July arrives, in this last of our years here
When you feel a little older
It will be an unforgettable day of your life

BLACK LIVES MATTER

Kansika

Black lives matter
People don't let anyone
Exploit your beauty

Look how amazing
The shades of black look on you

Black lives matter
Your own heroes, without you
We wouldn't have been inspired

Without you
Our environment wouldn't be diverse

Black lives matter
If you weren't here
Our world wouldn't have come this far

You've helped our lives
You've made this a better place

LIFE

Kansika

Life is like a book
You never know what will happen
Until you read it

Life is like a river
Sometimes it can be long or short
But it always has an end

Life is like a box of chocolates
You will never know how it will taste
Until you eat it

Life is a mixture of colours and feelings
Sometimes you will feel blue with sadness
Or yellow with happiness

Life is a series of random moments
Sometimes the moments are heart-breaking
Whereas some of the moments are gleeful

FRUIT

Divyansh

I'm a soft yellow banana
I'm creamy
I'm smooth and long
I'm sweet, sugary and delicious

I'm a big orange tangerine
I'm oval shaped and smooth
I'm sweet, juicy and delicious

Fruit: **Jessica** yr6

RACISM

Fareeha

We may look different
But we are as sweet as sugar
You spread rumours about me like bees collecting pollen
How would you feel?

Leaving behind nights of terror and fear
Tears rolling down our faces
All the places I go
I get judged like a book by its cover
How would you feel?

You may write about my skin colour in history
But you never write my good features
You treat us like less than
How would you feel?

God made us how we are
So why judge God's creation?
If someone judged your work of art
How would you feel?

LIFE

Rithuna

Spend time with the ones you love
You make mistakes
Everyone makes mistakes in life
Mistakes can happen
You may lose people that you love
Pour that love into the ones who need it
Happiness and joy can spread in our society

Fairy: **Maira** yr3

Hidden Secrets

Mithusa

Once upon a time, in a forgotten corner of the world, there stood an ancient mansion. It had been abandoned for centuries, its halls shaded in darkness and its secrets whispered through the wind. Many believed it was haunted and few dared to enter.

One stormy night, a brave adventurer named Alex found himself staring at the mansion. With nothing but a flickering flashlight, he went inside, his heart pounding with suspense. As Alex explored the mansion's ancient corridors, he discovered a hidden room tucked away behind a secret door. Inside he found a dusty old journal, its pages filled with weird symbols and old writing. It seemed to hold the key to unlocking the mansion's mysteries.

Driven by curiosity, Alex read the journal's riddles and followed its clues, leading him deeper into the mansion's secret. Each step brought him closer to uncovering the truth but also closer to the unknown dangers wandering around.

Finally, after a series of dangerous challenges, Alex reached the heart of the mansion. There, he discovered a hidden treasure, shimmering with untold riches. But as he reached out to take it, the mansion began to shake and crumble around him.

Alex raced through the collapsing mansion. As he reappeared into the stormy night, he glanced back at the ruins, his mind filled with wonder and a touch of sadness.

The mansion may have fallen but its mysteries would forever wander in his memory. And as Alex walked away, he couldn't help but wonder what other secrets were hidden in the world.

THE ABANDONED HOUSE

Mithusa

Once upon a time, in a small village nestled among towering trees, there stood an abandoned house. Its windows were broken, the paint on its walls was peeling and its garden was overgrown with weeds. The villagers believed that the house was haunted and avoided it at all costs.

One day, a curious young girl named Lily decided to explore the mysterious house. With her heart pounding, she pushed open the creaky front door and went inside. The air was musty and the only sound was the faint rustling of leaves outside.

As Lily cautiously made her way through the house, she discovered clues about its past. Old photographs, dusty books and faded letters hinted at a family that once called this place home. She felt a sense of sadness and wondered why the house had been abandoned.

In the attic, Lily stumbled upon a hidden journal. Its pages were filled with the dreams, hopes and fears of a young girl named Emily who had lived in the house long ago. Lily became captivated by Emily's story and was determined to uncover the truth behind the house's abandonment.

With each page she read, Lily unravelled the tale of a family torn apart by tragedy. She learned about a long lost treasure that was said to be hidden within the house. The treasure was rumoured to possess magical powers, capable of healing hearts and bringing happiness.

Haunted House: **Inaya** yr4

Driven by desire to bring closure to the family's story, Lily embarked on a quest to find the treasure. She deciphered riddles, solved puzzles and explored every nook and cranny of the house. Along the way, she encountered friendly spirits who guided her and offered words of encouragement.

Finally, after a series of challenges, Lily discovered the hidden chamber where the treasure awaited. In a dusty old chest, she found not only the treasure but also a letter from Emily herself. In her heartfelt words, Emily expressed her wish for the house to be filled with love and laughter once again.

With the treasure in her hands, Lily knew what she had to do. She gathered the villagers and shared the story of the abandoned house, its lost family and the power of forgiveness. Together, they restored the house to its former glory, turning it into a community centre where people could gather, share stories and find solace.

And so, the abandoned house was transformed from a place of mystery and fear into a symbol of hope and connection. Lily's bravery and determination had not only brought closure to a forgotten family, but had also brought new life to the entire world.

THE VALUES

Mahreen

One more story. This one is about two best friends who would look out for each other. They met during a convention to help with Maths and English. They had stuck together ever since. The end. Just joking! Their names were Klaus and Isadora, they were twelve years old, they were smart and funny, always laughing. Not today though. This story isn't about one of their adventures, it's about one of the hardships that they went through.

One day, Klaus saw a worried look on Isadora's face. He went up to her and asked her if she was alright. Isadora said that she was fine. Klaus knew that if she was fine, she would look cheerful however she was neither of those things today, which was unusual. As the days went by, he kept asking this question until she gave in and told him what was going on. Isadora felt as if she couldn't keep it in anymore because it was now getting out of control. She told Klaus that she was being bullied because she was best friends with a boy. Klaus offered to help her tell someone about the situation but she said no. She told him that if anyone found out that she had told on the bullies, she might start being blackmailed by them. Klaus told

Isadora that she should have no fear because he would always be beside her to support her.

So they both went hand in hand to tell the head teacher what was going on. As a result, the parents of those bullies were told and the bullies themselves had to undergo reflection with the school counsellor.

There is a moral to this story too. That Klaus showed concern, kindness and resilience towards Isadora. She showed confidence and communicated whilst dealing with the situation. As for the bullies, they had to learn to reflect on what they had done and change their attitude and behaviour.

Nobody should be treated like this, ever. The values we have at our school are represented in this story and give examples of how we should behave.

Thank you for reading our book and our poems and stories!

9 781835 632864